# THE SPANISH MUSTANG

By Ellen Frazel

Consultant:
Dr. Emily Leuthner
DVM, MS, DACVIM
Country View Veterinary Service
Oregon, Wisc.

BELLWETHER MEDIA • MINNEAPOLIS, MN

Jump into the cockpit and take flight with Pilot Books. Your journey will take you on high-energy adventures as you learn about all that is wild, weird, fascinating, and fun!

This edition first published in 2012 by Bellwether Media, Inc.

No part of this publication may be reproduced in whole or in part without written permission of the publisher. For information regarding permission, write to Bellwether Media, Inc., Attention: Permissions Department, 5357 Penn Avenue South, Minneapolis, MN 55419.

Library of Congress Cataloging-in-Publication Data

Frazel, Ellen.
The spanish mustang / by Ellen Frazel.
   p. cm. – (Pilot books. Horse breed roundup)
Includes bibliographical references and index.
Summary: "Engaging images accompany information about the Spanish Mustang. The combination of high-interest subject matter and narrative text is intended for students in grades 3 through 7"–Provided by publisher.
ISBN 978-1-60014-659-6 (hardcover : alk. paper)
1. Mustang–Juvenile literature. I. Title.
SF293.M9F73 2012
636.1'3–dc22                                              2011014291

Printed in the United States of America, North Mankato, MN.

080111      1187

# CONTENTS

# The Spanish Mustang

A horse and rider have been traveling for miles over mountains and across deserts. The horse has remained strong throughout the entire journey. By the end of the day, the horse and rider have traveled 100 miles (161 kilometers)! The horse is a Spanish Mustang. This breed is famous for its **endurance**.

Spanish Mustangs have a tough, independent **temperament**. They are **hardy** horses that are built to travel long distances. Spanish Mustangs stand between 13 and 15 **hands** tall. This is between 52 and 60 inches (132 and 152 centimeters). They are not very muscular. However, they have **symmetrical** bodies and short, sturdy backs that help them carry heavy loads. Their legs and feet are strong for long journeys.

**Enduring Legacy**
The Spanish Mustang is called "the horse with a heritage" because of its rich history and the many hardships it has endured.

Spanish Mustangs come in many different coat colors. The most common colors are black, gray, and reddish brown shades like chestnut and bay. Some coats can be a tan color called buckskin, a cream color called cremello, or a very pale yellow called isabelline. All Spanish Mustangs have short, rugged hair. However, their flowing tails and manes add a gentle beauty to their look.

Spanish Mustangs also have small mouths and crescent-shaped nostrils. Their eyes are large and set deep into their foreheads. Their curved ears and long, arched necks give them a graceful appearance.

# From Spanish Explorers to Native Americans

In the late 1400s, Christopher Columbus began to explore the Americas. Europeans called these lands "the New World." He first landed on several islands in the **Caribbean**. In 1493, he took his second voyage to the New World. He brought Spanish horses with him. These horses are the direct **ancestors** of the Spanish Mustang.

After that voyage, every ship carried Spanish horses to the New World. The Spanish set up farms where their animals could breed. The Andalusian, the Jennet, and the Barb are a few of the horse breeds that were brought to these farms. Spanish **conquistadors** continued to explore and bring horses to the New World throughout the 1500s and 1600s.

## Best of the Best

In the 1400s, Spain was known around the world for its horses. The Spanish had spent hundreds of years breeding the best characteristics. The Andalusian was considered the strongest, toughest horse breed in Spain.

**Andalusian**

A Catholic priest named Eusebio Kino ran one horse farm in Mexico. In the 1600s, he worked to spread Christianity to the Native Americans there. He tried to win their trust by giving them horses. Some Native Americans did not respond well to Kino's efforts. The Apache stole horses from Kino and other Spaniards. Some horses also escaped. These wild horses became **feral** Mustangs. Many people confuse the Spanish Mustang with this horse. Though they are closely related, the Spanish Mustang was never wild.

## Wild Brothers and Sisters

Feral Mustang herds still roam the United States today. Some show characteristics of different tamed breeds such as the Thoroughbred and the American Quarter Horse.

feral Mustangs

The Spanish horses spread throughout the New World. They earned a reputation as hardy horses. While other European horses were getting sick or dying, the Spanish horses **adapted** well to the unfamiliar land. The harsh conditions made them very tough. They could work longer and travel farther than other horses. They covered long distances without much food, water, or rest.

These horses changed the lives of the Native Americans. They made it easier for tribes to travel and gather food. The Apache were responsible for much of the development of the Spanish Mustang. They traded their Spanish horses with many other tribes. This spread the horses all over the American West. The Apache and other tribes chose the strongest Spanish horses to have **foals**. In the 1700s, the Spanish Mustang started to emerge as a specific breed.

## Mustang Mail

Spanish Mustangs were used in the Pony Express. This was a mail service that went from Missouri to California in 1860. The Pony Express crossed the Great Plains, the Rocky Mountains, and the Sierra Nevada.

Spanish Mustangs helped the Native Americans fight
for their land in the 1800s. American **settlers** had begun
to move west in search of gold and farmland. They went to
war with the Native Americans to drive them from their land.
The United States **cavalry** had guns and other advanced
weapons. The Native Americans had the strength and speed
of their horses. Eventually, the U.S. cavalry started riding
Spanish Mustangs to keep up in battle. The Native Americans
could not win.

The American settlers took over both the West and the Spanish Mustang. They used the breed to help build the United States. Thousands of Spanish Mustangs worked on farms and as **cow horses**. However, other horse breeds came to the United States in the late 1800s. Spanish Mustangs became less popular. The U.S. government even killed thousands of Spanish Mustangs because they were thought to be too wild. By 1920, the breed was almost **extinct**. Robert and Ferdinand Brislawn wanted to save the breed. They formed the Spanish Mustang Registry, Inc. in 1957.

# Speed, Skill, and Endurance

The number of Spanish Mustangs is still very low today. They are almost extinct in Spain. In the U.S., they are listed as a **critical horse breed**. Despite their low numbers, Spanish Mustangs appear in events like team penning, reining, and gymkhana.

In team penning, a team of three riders and their horses herd cattle. They try to separate three marked cattle from a large group and lead them into a pen. In reining, a horse performs a series of circles, spins, and stops at the command of its rider. Gymkhana refers to racing events that involve patterns. Horses race in patterns around barrels, poles, flags, or other obstacles. The fastest horses are the winners!

## Native American Games

Gymkhana is also called O-Mok-See. This is a Native American phrase that means "games on horseback." Some of the activities are thought to come from traditional war dances performed by the Blackfoot tribe. They rode their horses around in circles before going into battle.

# Famous Spanish Mustangs

## Chief Yellow Fox

Chief Yellow Fox won several endurance riding awards in 1989. He was the Midwest Region Overall Grand Champion of the American Endurance Ride Conference. He also won the Jim Jones Stallion Award for 1,500 miles (2,410 kilometers) traveled in a year.

## Little Hawk

Little Hawk won the Conquistador of Games title in 2001 from the Spanish Mustang Registry, Inc. He was the first horse to collect enough points in one season to earn that award.

## Geronimo's Warrior

In 2004, Geronimo's Warrior won the Jim Jones Stallion Award for the fifth year in a row. He had incredible endurance and was able to travel hundreds of miles every year. He logged his 10,000th mile in 2004!

Spanish Mustangs are still known for their incredible endurance. Many people choose them for **endurance riding**. The Tevis Cup is a 100-mile (161-kilometer) endurance ride across part of California. It has been held since 1955 and is the oldest endurance ride in the country.

The Tevis Cup trail winds up rocky mountainsides and descends into valleys. It is the roughest endurance course in the United States. A horse and rider get a silver Completion Award Buckle if they complete the trail in 24 hours. Only about half of the riders who set out on the trail make it to the finish line in this time. Spanish Mustangs often do well in the Tevis Cup. Their history has prepared them to endure this rigorous trek. Both on and off the trail, they show the strength that has helped them survive the past and succeed today.

# Glossary

**adapted**—adjusted to new and changing conditions

**ancestors**—family members who lived long ago

**Caribbean**—the area west of the Atlantic Ocean and between North and South America; the Caribbean has many islands.

**cavalry**—military troops on horseback

**conquistadors**—Spanish explorers who sailed to the Americas between the 1400s and 1600s

**cow horses**—horses that herd cows

**critical horse breed**—a breed of horse that is in danger of becoming extinct

**endurance**—the ability to do something for a long time

**endurance riding**—a sport in which riders and their horses travel long distances

**extinct**—no longer existing

**feral**—untamed; feral animals have not been trained by humans.

**foals**—young horses; foals are under one year old.

**hands**—the units used to measure the height of a horse; one hand is equal to 4 inches (10.2 centimeters).

**hardy**—having the physical strength to endure harsh conditions

**settlers**—people who come to live in a new land

**symmetrical**—having equal-sized, corresponding parts; Spanish Mustangs have very symmetrical bodies.

**temperament**—personality or nature; the Spanish Mustang has a tough, independent temperament.

# To Learn More

## At the Library

Criscione, Rachel Damon. *The Mustang*. New York, N.Y.: The Rosen Publishing Group's PowerKids Press, 2007.

Dutson, Judith. *Horse Breeds of North America*. North Adams, Mass.: Storey Pub., 2006.

Parise-Peterson, Amanda. *The Spanish Mustang*. Mankato, Minn.: Edge Books, 2006.

## On the Web

Learning more about
Spanish Mustangs is as easy as 1, 2, 3.

1. Go to www.factsurfer.com.

2. Enter "Spanish Mustangs" into the search box.

3. Click the "Surf" button and you will see a list of related Web sites.

With factsurfer.com, finding more information
is just a click away.

# Index

The images in this book are reproduced through the courtesy of: J-L Klein & M-L Hubert / Photolibrary, front cover, pp. 18-19; Masterfile, pp. 4-5; Mark J. Barrett / KimballStock, pp. 6-7; Grebler M / Photolibrary, pp. 8-9; franzfoto.com / Alamy, pp. 10-11; Juniors Bildarchiv / Alamy, pp. 12-13; SuperStock / Getty Images, p. 14; Winthrop Brookhouse, p. 15; Steve Blake, pp. 16-17; Lynne Glazer, pp. 20-21.